I0407629

Table of Contents

What is consulting?

Consultants are people who specialize in helping clients resolve their company's most urgent problems, issues, or projects. They work across a huge range of roles and industries and share their gift of analyzing information and identifying the best path for each company to take.

Consulting is the business of giving expert advice to other professionals. While it sounds simple enough, your success as a consultant is dependent not only on having expertise in the industry but also a natural ability to solve problems and make decisions.

Consulting can be categorized into two main sectors:

Strategy consulting

Strategy consultants focus their efforts on beating the competition and elevating business profit. When clients are struggling with a specific business direction, strategy consultants address the question of how to do it.

Management consulting

Management consultants are responsible for the process of developing or improving business strategies. Management consultants often specialize in a particular industry, some of which include:

- Human resources consulting: An HR consultant addresses human resources tasks and processes in the overall business model.

- IT consulting: An IT consultant specializes in optimizing information systems and has a sound understanding of technology services. Sometimes referred to as technology consultants, they work with clients to improve the structure and efficiency of technical systems.
- Health care consulting: A health-care consultant is responsible for identifying efficiency gaps to improve the structure and operation of health-care organizations.

What does a consultant do?

Consultants are hired for a variety of reasons that span from implementing simple changes to completely overhauling current business systems.

Here are five reasons you might be hired as a consultant:

- To teach expertise Many businesses lack expertise in certain departments and need a consultant's help to drive growth. In these situations, you're hired to come in and educate staff on processes that elevate their business.
- To identify problems Using your expertise, you may be hired to identify problems in a business model. If you are hired in this scenario, it's your

responsibility to identify weaknesses that are bogging down the business.

- To improve processes Some businesses can identify the problem but can't find the solution. In these situations, a business hires you to create a plan to remedy key pain points.
- To execute new methods While some consulting businesses advise, others actually implement. A business may ask for your counsel regarding the health of its business, but you may also follow up with the implementation of your suggested plan.
- To oversee business development When entrepreneurs decide to open a business, they might ask a consultant to oversee their business's

development. Depending on your niche, you might advise on entering the market or provide financial oversight.

Whether you are ready to open your consulting business tomorrow or you are just beginning to think about it, it's important to understand what consultants specialize in so you can define where you fit in the market.

What are the pros and cons of becoming a consultant?

Like any career, consultant jobs come with highs and lows. Every business you work with will provide you with different, and often contrasting, experiences.

The pros

It's challenging and rewarding

When you're a consultant, no two days are the same. Every day may throw new challenges your way! These challenges pay off, though. There's nothing that really compares to dragging a business out of a slump and setting it up for the future. Plus, the success you have with each project contributes directly to your personal brand.

It's fast-paced and you get a sense of freedom

Consultants are often hired in desperate times to rectify a serious situation. Working in such a fast-paced career is perfect for someone who enjoys a challenge, and a sense of freedom traveling from one business to the next.

You'll constantly be learning

Consultants are experts in their field. To maintain this badge, they must always be learning and adapting to new trends in their industry. This enables them to help businesses develop techniques to stay ahead of their competitors.

The cons

Income instability

There is a certain air of instability when working as a consultant. You never really know when or where your services are going to be required next. For people who rely on very steady income, being a consultant full-time may lead to some stressful days.

There's constant change

You might be required to uproot and move across state, or even across the country at short notice. If you've got other responsibilities, like children, this might not be a realistic option for you.

Weighing the pros and cons should allow you to understand if a consulting role is best for you. If you're not sure, you can always try it out as a side gig first!

Thing to consider before starting a consulting business

Starting an own business is about taking a huge step forward in both career and professional life. Taking such a step is not easy and definitely takes a lot of courage. Since it is such an important leap, aspiring entrepreneurs need to be certain they have got everything under control and are 100% ready for their new venture. The same goes for consultants seeking to start their own consulting business.

1. Check the Market

As you are aware, consultancy is such a broad term. You can't simply choose to be "a consultant". In fact, a consultant is not a protected profession, meaning that any professional can call himself/herself a consultant. Key is therefore to choose a specific segment of the consulting industry and making it your specialty. Typical areas consultants can work in include: strategy;

finance, risk & compliance; IT, digital and technology; human resources, operations management & supply chain; organisation & management; and mergers & acquisitions. These are some of the most prominent types of consulting, widely spread and in high demand. But, how can you choose which way to go? If you're not choosing based on personal preference, you should explore the market by checking the statistics and using data analysis, if possible. See which services are most needed and what kind of consultants are currently in demand. For instance, at the time of writing, consultants with expertise in cybersecurity and data science are in high-demand on the back of booming demand in the segments. Consultancy buyers don't want a consultant "for everything". They want an expert in the niche and someone who specialises to be the best in exactly what they need. In other words, you need to define your path and be certain which way you want to go.

2.Rethinking Consulting Skills

You made the first step, which is selecting a specific consultancy niche. Now it's time to consider your skills and expertise. The question is: can you do it? Your task is to do the homework and gather information about the specific skill set you need in order to rightfully do the consultancy job you've chosen. We are not talking about the official consultancy education, degrees, and certificates. We are talking about the applicable practical knowledge. Ask yourself, can you: asses the client's problems? Design an action plan? Help a client build capacity? Tailor a change management plan? Lead a programme transition including navigating change? Deliver on results including the business case?

Analyse your niche, learn what you need to know, work on your skills based on what the market requires and grow to be better every day.

3. Structuring pricing

For many beginners, structuring the pricing of their services can be a puzzle. You're only just getting started and you fear to stand shoulder to shoulder with your competition. Pricing is key in consulting, with the fee charged for consultants currently under high scrutiny from clients. A growing number of tools are creating more transparency in consultant fees, meanwhile the rise of independent consultants in line with the gig-economy means that fees are under pressure.

When structuring your pricing, remember:

- you need to be cost-effective for companies who hire you; that is, less expensive than them hiring a long-term specialist;
- don't underprice; value your knowledge;
- be specific; create a pricing guide to help you decide on the exact pricing for each specific project and client.

4. Keep track of the metrics

It's important to start keeping track of the success of your consulting business the moment it starts. It will help you gain insight on your efficiency, productiveness and client satisfaction. Consequently, it will help you learn, develop, improve and grow to be even better. Therefore, before starting a consulting business, make sure to learn all about the metrics for your niche. For example:

- Leads generated: the number of clients leads generated by marketing and business development
- Utilisation rate: the number of hours working for a client, also known as chargeability or billable hours
- Customer satisfaction: how satisfied clients are with the engagement delivered by a consultant
- Repeat business rate: the number of repeat clients in a consultants'

portfolio, a measure of client
satisfaction

- Gross margin: a key performance
  indicator to highlight the profitability
  of consulting operations

When preparing to start a consulting
business, you need to be aware of the value
of data analysis and metrics. Start keeping
track from day one as it can down the line
provide extremely relevant information.

5. Reach out

Before going all in, try connecting with
potential clients and even future colleagues
and making as many new contacts as
possible. Build your LinkedIn profile and
look for others from the same industry.
Further, research what clients have to say
about the consulting industry and what

types of services are being hired by them. This will help you stay informed and up-to-date on the latest consultancy-related information and happenings. It will also allow you to have someone to ask for an advice, an opinion or simply to talk about your progress.

How to Start a Consulting Business Step-by-Step Guide

1. Choose your niche

2. Define your services

3. Write a business plan

4. Hire an experienced business attorney

5. Decide your legal business structure

6. Set up accounting and bookkeeping

7. Assess your finances

8. Develop your brand identity

9. Fill in the business blanks

10. Crunch the numbers

11. Build an online presence

12. Create a sales plan

13. Spread the word

14. Find partners or investors

15. Find the right help

STEP 1

Choose your niche

One of the keys to success as a consultant is identifying and embracing your niche.

You know a lot about marketing or finance or.whatever. But so do a lot of other folks.

When starting a consulting business, it will be much easier to differentiate yourself from all of those other generalized consultants, especially over the long term, if you specialize. Think about it. If you had lung cancer, would you go to a general practitioner or an oncologist specializing in lung cancer? You'd go to that lung cancer specialist because they're the best chance you've got to solve your unique problem.

The same is true for businesses that need consultants. They will spend their hard-earned money to pay your fees. And, they want some degree of assurance that they're going to get their money's worth. A consultant is an expert in a particular field. Knowing that you're an expert in their issue will boost their confidence in your ability to get the job done. Consultants who are specialists will appear most qualified to help and will be most appealing to the clients and potential clients with those challenges. Dana Anspach, certified financial planner, consultant, and retirement expert, explains:

Don't try to offer something to everyone. You will be a far more successful consultant by applying your expertise to a niche market that needs what you have to offer. In this way, you can tailor your services, so they add value to a specific group of people or businesses. You may find that your niche reveals itself effortlessly. It may be the area in which you have the most expertise in your field. Or, it may be the niche that you find most fun and exciting.

For example, in my opinion definitive guide on how to start a successful clothing brand or clothing line suggested that aspiring apparel entrepreneurs choose their niche. It's impossible and expensive to please everyone and do everything.

You have the same challenge: how to focus your energies on an area (or multiple areas) where your strengths and experience can bring the most value to your clients and potential clients.

But, if you're struggling to identify what your niche or specialty might be, consider these techniques for narrowing it down:

- Identify any underserved specialties in your field.
- Consider what specialties will continue to be underserved by a suitable consultant over the long term.
- Determine which areas in your field clients and potential clients struggle with the most.
- Ask yourself if your unique background and niche expertise provide you with a rare knowledge area not easily found in the job market.
- You've probably informally helped friends already to solve their business problems and pain points. What areas have you focused on when working with your friends?

- Is your consulting business limited to helping clients in the United States, or will you provide services to clients worldwide?
- Whatever niche you choose, don't make the mistake of trying to be the right fit for every client. A good consultant determines a specific calling and then markets their skills to that niche audience.

Most likely, you've already taken steps to unearth the areas where you're a true expert. Here's how Mandi Ellefson, CEO of The Hands-Off CEO, started her consulting business:

I had a design company where we did branding and web design. I spent so much time working in the business that it really couldn't work for me. I felt like a slave for the business. I wanted to work on the business to scale it.

I was not able to remove myself from the business at all. It was dependent on me and I really wanted this company to be generating income without me. But it wasn't anywhere close to doing so. So I had to figure out how to scale the business without working more in the business. In the process of doing that, I had a lot of success and started building processes around how to do that. And as a result, I sold my company and started a consulting business to help others do the same thing.

Maybe what you're already doing inspires you. Or you can look at the following areas when starting a consulting business:

- Accounting. Every business needs accounting. Accounting consultants help companies with financial needs.
- Advertising. Help businesses with their online and offline advertising campaigns.
- Auditing. Help clients and potential audit their financial, human resources, or legal records.
- Coaching other consultants. Suppose you've been successful as a consultant. In that case, you can also consider a consulting business that offers a coaching program for consultants, including expert advice on starting and growing their consulting firms.
- General business. Coaching and general business consulting to help business owners overcome a variety

of obstacles. You can even set up a formal or informal coaching program for clients and prospective clients.

- Business writing. Too many business owners are poor writers. Successful consultants can often teach business owners to write better, or shadow write for them.
- Career consulting. Many people are in transition, and career consultants will always be in demand to help people find the next best thing.
- Communications. Helping teams to better communicate with each other and assisting the companies to better communicate with the market.
- Computer programmer or technology. Helping clients and potential clients with software and/or hardware issues.

- Editorial services. Helping businesses to create newsletters, annual reports, press releases, etc.
- Gardening. People and businesses are increasingly interested in building comfortable gardens and landscaping. Gardening consultants are in high demand.
- Grantsmanship. Helping organizations, and especially nonprofits, write grant proposals.
- Human resources consulting or executive search consulting. Many small businesses can't afford to hire full-time HR staff. HR consultants can help to fill that gap.
- Insurance. Everyone needs insurance, but it's tough to know what to get and how much to pay. That's where good consultants can help.

- Marketing. Few business owners understand marketing. Yet, they still need to create a marketing plan, develop strategies, and execute. Marketing consulting can help many companies, especially small businesses, with marketing campaigns and marketing strategies, including social media marketing efforts and email marketing.
- Payroll management. Provide payroll services to small businesses.
- Public relations. Few business owners know how to engage the media. Experienced media consultants can shine a brighter light and help companies break out from the crowd.
- Publishing. Helping individuals and organizations launch podcasts, newsletters, books, magazines, etc.

- Supply chain management. Help clients understand how to manage their vendors and supply chain best. This is especially useful if your clients manufacture products from parts sourced from other businesses.
- Taxes. Everyone must pay taxes. A tax consultant helps businesses pay the least amount of tax possible when the company files its tax return.
- Writing services. Helping individuals and businesses with all types of copywriting.

Communicating directly to the leads who need your area of expertise will deliver the best results.

And if you feel that you need to round out your experience and skillset with special training, take advantage of opportunities to improve your skillset. This is true even if you're an expert in your field. You may be a good consultant, but depending on the consulting business model you select, you may need special training to give clients and potential clients certain types of expert advice.

While you might be an expert in your specific field, a successful consulting business may require you to develop particular skills. For example, you might be called upon to speak publicly, train others, identify problems and pain points in teams or processes, analyze and present data, and offer written or verbal.

You'll also need to find a consulting business model that fits your skills and goals.

The solo consultant model

As a solo consultant, you'll work closely with your clients and complete the project and all deliverables yourself. If you want a lean and flexible consulting business, this is a good model for you.

The consulting firm model

When you open a consulting firm, you are responsible for running the firm and working on client projects. This will give you additional responsibilities and allow you to hire other consultants and support staff to create and grow a more significant consulting business. If you don't like managing people or focusing on the daily activities of running a business, this may not be the ideal consulting business model for you.

The productized consulting model

In this variation, instead of providing direct consulting services as a solo consultant or through a consulting firm, you create products based on your knowledge. For example, you can create a process and learning program that you sell to others for a fixed fee or a monthly price. This model allows you to reduce your day-to-day work and create a saleable asset that works while you sleep.

The hybrid consulting model

This is a mixture of two or more of the above consulting models. You pick and choose what you want to do and build a consulting business that focuses on those things. Today, many successful consulting firms follow a hybrid consulting model.

STEP 2

Define your consulting services

Consulting is a broad and potentially vague concept.But clients and potential clients don't pay money for vague promises. If you want your business to succeed, you need to show new clients and potential clients the specific consulting service you will offer and deliver. That begins with you defining your services and deliverables and your consulting business model when starting a consulting business.You can start by assessing your skillset and brainstorming the general consulting services you'd like to offer. But, you must nail down the specifics of your consulting offer before you work with any clients.

This is vital for three reasons:

You need to articulate your consulting service to potential clients to convince them that your services are valuable.

You'll need to charge fees that let you run a sustainable business.

Specificity helps to set realistic expectations for your clients and potential clients.

This last point benefits both you and your clients. Your clients can make comfortable, informed decisions. And you can avoid clients taking advantage of you.

Tim Berry, entrepreneur and business planning evangelist, advises:

Expect scope creep clients asking for more after they've agreed on deliverables and price and deal with it delicately, suggesting the extra work needs extra fees. This is one of the toughest problems you'll have, and there are no easy solutions.

While you can't prevent "scope creep" entirely, being clear about exactly what a client is paying for upfront (and getting it in writing) will help to set realistic, workable boundaries both parties can agree to. And, importantly, this will also clearly define the value proposition for your consulting business.

You should also understand why clients hire consultants. Here are some of the reasons that businesses hire consultants:

Businesses hire consultants because of his or her expertise. Suppose a company is raising funding or adopting a new software system. In that case, it pays for them to hire a specialist who has raised millions or has already implemented the same software system.

Businesses hire consultants to supplement their staff. Sometimes, businesses use consultants instead of hiring full-time or part-time employees. They do this because they don't need to pay consultants' benefits, and some projects may be temporary.

Businesses hire consultants to identify problems. It's not uncommon for employees to struggle to resolve an issue inside an organization. Having seen a similar situation across many organizations, an experienced consultant might have the necessary expertise to help.

Businesses hire consultants to promote change. Often, companies get stuck trying to change their internal organization.

Outside consultants are often used to facilitate the transition.

Businesses hire consultants to teach. Training programs, retraining programs, technical software implementation, and other areas require specialized skills that only experienced consultants offer.

Businesses hire consultants to make tough decisions. If a company needs to downsize, they will often bring in consultants to make the tough decisions to deflect blame for letting people go.

Businesses hire consultants to influence important decision-makers at other companies. For example, if you're trying to reach a deal with another company and find a consultant that knows that company well, the consultant may be the X factor in putting the deal together.

Businesses hire consultants for ideation. Sometimes, a company hits a rough patch and has a hard time finding new ideas. Consultants can help bring new energy to the business and help ideate products and services.

Businesses hire consultants to create new companies and products. Some specialized consultants help others create (or buy) new companies and products and services.

As a consultant, your services and deliverables are the core of your business. Once you know what you'll be offering to your new clients and your target market, you're ready to move on to the next step writing a business plan.

STEP 3

Write a business plan

Once you choose your niche and define your services, it's time to write a business plan. People make many mistakes when they start a new business and rush into things before considering the essential aspects of their business. Although writing a business plan isn't mandatory, it can help you crystallize your ideas and avoid many mistakes. Studies show that entrepreneurs who take the time to write a business plan when starting a business are 2.5 times more likely to follow through and get their business off the ground. The work that goes into creating a business plan also helps new entrepreneurs build skills that will be invaluable later. But, don't get obsessed about getting every detail right in your business plan.You don't even need to write a traditional 100-page business plan. Several compelling business plan frameworks can help you write a one page business plan. For insights and free downloadable business plan templates, read this definitive guide to writing a business plan.

STEP 4

Hire an experienced business attorney

Most consultants dread having to talk with and hire a business lawyer when starting a consulting business. Some fear they'll end up paying exorbitant legal fees or that they'll receive bad advice that will destroy their business. Others agonize over how to find a reasonably priced, competent business lawyer.

Here's what you need to know to hire a good lawyer for your new consulting business.

Hire a lawyer who adds value

We've met and have sat across the table from many lawyers who are deal-killers. Overzealous and often inexperienced, they focus on the wrong issues and forget that their client needs the deal to move forward. When you talk with lawyers you're considering hiring, ask them about one or two complicated negotiations and how they overcame obstacles.

Don't make price your main criteria for hiring a lawyer.

Often, the least expensive lawyers are also less experienced especially in the areas where you may need help. Paying a cheaper hourly rate might feel good initially, but in the end, you may end up paying far more than if you hired an experienced (more expensive) lawyer in the first place. Make sure your lawyer is familiar with the peculiarities of consulting businesses and has experience representing other consultants. Also be clear about your budget and expectations. Your lawyer should understand that your budget is limited and that they should not waste that budget on irrelevant details.

Hire a lawyer responsive to your needs

Your lawyer won't be very helpful if they're not responsive when you need them. Because many deals and transactions are time-sensitive, be sure that your lawyer will be there for you when you need them. After all, a client isn't going to keep waiting for weeks for your lawyer to review a proposed consulting contract.

When to hire a lawyer

Typically, the best time to start a relationship with a lawyer is before you start your consulting business. Too many people make the mistake of forming a company and reaching an agreement among co-founders without consulting a lawyer. In some cases, some co-founders leave retaining their interest and the rest are left to try to make the business work. A good lawyer will help you find the proper business structure for the business and split ownership interests in ways that will protect everyone and give you flexibility in the future.

STEP 5

Decide your legal business structure

Before starting your consulting business, you need to decide on the type of entity you need to register.Your legal business structure affects everything, from how you file your taxes to your personal liability and whether you need to comply with any special additional requirements at the local, state, or national levels.

There are many different types of legal business structures for various business entities. For new business owners, choosing the best business entity for your business can feel overwhelming.

Don't rush yourself into deciding to register your business immediately. For example, while a sole proprietorship might be quick and inexpensive in the short term, it might expose you to more risk, create an unfavorable tax treatment, and create problems for you in the long term. A limited liability company (LLC) might make more sense for most consulting businesses. Spend some time reading about each possible entity your business might fit into. Consider which business structure is most helpful for your business and how each business structure can help you accomplish your professional and personal goals.

What are the four types of business entities?

- A sole proprietorship is the most basic business entity. A sole proprietorship means that one person is solely responsible for business profits and debts.
- A partnership is a shared responsibility between two or more people who hold personal liability for a business.
- Limited Liability Company (LLC) is a business structure that permits owners, partners, or shareholders to limit personal liability but still includes tax and flexibility benefits associated with a partnership.
- A corporation is an entity legally considered separate from its owners. That means that corporations are

permitted to own property, be held liable, pay taxes, and enter contracts.

Be sure to look at which entity will work best for your current needs while still considering any future business goals. Remember that most states require you to register your consulting firm with the secretary of state or county clerk in the county in which you operate your business if the trade name under which you run your business differs from the legal business name of your business. For example, suppose your registered company is a limited liability company (LLC), and the legal business name is Three Brothers, LLC. In that case, you cannot operate that business lawfully in most states if you're selling products under the trade name Three Tigers. That's because the registered business name, and your trade name, are different. Fortunately, this is not a complex problem to overcome. You can simply register your actual trade name with your state (and or local government) by filing a "doing business as" (DBA) certificate. DBAs are also commonly called "assumed name," "fictitious business name," or "trade name.

STEP 6

Set up business accounting and bookkeeping

To keep track of your finances when starting a consulting business, you'll need to set up a bookkeeping and accounting system. This is important so that you understand your business's cash flow and will also be necessary for tax-filing purposes.

Here's what you need to know about accounting and bookkeeping for your new consulting business.

Business accounting is how your business records, organizes, interprets, and presents its financial information. Accountants analyze the financial condition of a business to help the business owner make better decisions.

Bookkeeping is the recording, organization, storage, and retrieval of financial information related to your business.

Accounting and bookkeeping do overlap. The main difference between the two is that bookkeeping is how you record and categorize financial information, whereas accounting puts the information to use through analysis, strategy, and tax planning.

Start by hiring a bookkeeper

A great bookkeeper is not the same as an accountant. Many business owners hire a bookkeeper with some simple goals in mind: keep me organized, get my bills paid, and prepare for the work that will be handed to the accountant. Typically, bookkeepers are less expensive than CPAs (certified public accountants) and can be trusted to record and organize your day-to-day business transactions, keep your business bank account balanced, produce simple reports, and assist with keeping your financial records in order.

Many consulting businesses will use an outside bookkeeper, paid hourly, who is in the office regularly to handle all entries, pay all the bills, and manage invoicing and receivables. Having help with this aspect of managing a small company can be indispensable, and the time it can free for a busy owner, invaluable.

And, importantly, a bookkeeper doesn't have to share your office space with you. They can efficiently work remotely or visit your office one day every few weeks.

A bookkeeper can help you organize your financial information

Any business from the smallest of hot dog stands to the largest of public companies creates data. Sales data, inventory data, employee data, customer data. The list is endless. And like any kind of data, if data is not organized and accessible, it is entirely useless. You will find this to be especially relevant to your consulting business. With accounting data, this is doubly true, and the speed at which a small business can fall behind can be breathtaking. Even a few weeks of unrecorded sales transactions or a month of un-mailed invoices can quickly swamp a small business, destroy cash flow, and put it out of business faster than you can spell IRS. A good bookkeeper can help you set up a filing system, keep bills organized and paid on time, ensure that customer invoices go out promptly, and put plans in place that will force you to do these things in a disciplined and organized way.

A good bookkeeper can also help you set up and track an invoice financing loan if you need to accelerate payments by clients but clients insist on paying 30 or more days after they get your invoice.

Review your accounting processes annually and make adjustments

Do not underestimate the importance of a periodic review of your bookkeeping, accounting, and tax strategies. At your peril, you neglect to take a hard look at the systems you have in place and the people managing those systems.

Are you doing your accounting most productively and cost-effectively? Does your CPA have the right level of industry knowledge to advise? Does your tax-preparer have the skills and expertise to keep you (and your investors) on the right side of the law? And finally (the big one), can you find ways to reduce your expenses while maintaining high-quality controls? Take the time to reconsider your overall accounting strategy and find ways to strengthen and improve it.

STEP 7

Assess your finances

When you start a new consulting business, assessing your finances is crucial. These numbers include tracking your sales and profits - but an innovative business will need to account for much more than sales alone.

Here's what you need to know about business finance and how to crunch the numbers for your new business.

Business finance uses your company's financial information to help you manage your money and make your business operations profitable and sustainable. You have many business financing options. That's important because you need to determine how you're going to fund your new business and how you'll grow it. If you don't understand the numbers, you'll have a tough time building a sustainable, profitable business. Be extra careful to conserve your funds when starting a business. Don't overspend. Some purchases will be necessary and will make sense for your business, but others, like expensive and unnecessary equipment, will threaten your small business's survivability. The good news is that most successful consultants can run their businesses without considerable costs in the beginning until they build a book of clients and can spend a bit more on equipment and supplies.

To keep track of your finances, you'll need to set up a bookkeeping and accounting system. We talked about this above. This is important so that you understand your business's cash flow and will also be necessary for tax-filing purposes. Your accounting and bookkeeping system will include income, expenses, capital expenditures, profit, loss, EBITDA, etc.

STEP 8

Develop your brand identity

Brands are not just for big corporations. Brands are even more critical for small businesses like independent consultants. Branding provides a reassuring level of professionalism that very small operations may struggle to establish .So, don't think you can afford to leave your brand identity to chance. It's hard to build a successful consulting business unless you take branding seriously.

Your brand is your company's public identity. Ideally, your brand should embody the best (and most essential) attributes of your company. The importance of your brand identity cannot be understated. Consultants must be viewed as credible experts to gain their clients' trust. Weak brand identity will undermine that credibility. Mandi Ellefson, a successful consultant helping small businesses to improve their business growth and revenues, explains:

We believe that good design is good business. But most business owners are not designers. They're not marketers. They may or may not know what good design is but they're not necessarily the person who can create it.

You absolutely have to elevate your brand. If you want to charge higher fees, if you want to attract a certain level of clients, you have to project a certain image. And if you have a sloppy website, one that looks like it's from the 1990s and a nasty pixelated logo, you won't attract good clients or project a professional image.

Good design is good business, not just for your clients but also for you. The Forbes Coaches Council explains it this way:

Being a credible mentor for clients is key to achieving success in the industry. Your reputation relies on whether your clients trust in you and the services that you offer them. In other words, you've got to walk the walk and talk the talk. This includes things like a custom email address and a domain that matches your consulting business's name. People think less of consultants that use Gmail or Yahoo email addresses. We asked Mandi Ellefson, who often works with consultants and agencies, to illustrate with an example:

I work with B2B service businesses and lots of agencies with revenues in the multiple six and seven-figure range. One of their biggest challenges is attracting better quality clients. They typically have a pretty good number of clients, but they want to attract better quality clients. In order to do that, you need to be able to sell with your current skills your current assets. But if you're currently selling $10,000 projects, what will it take to be able to sell a $20,000 dollar project? To be able to sell a $20,000 dollar project, you have to be able to articulate the value in a different way and design can help you do that.

So, before you hit up your first networking event, ask yourself these critical questions:

- What identity/personality do I want my consulting brand to project?
- Who will want or need my services?
- What can consulting clients get from my services that they can't get from other consultants?
- What can clients get from working with me that they can't get from other consulting businesses?
- What are my brand values?
- What is the essential part of my clients' experience?

Your answers to these questions (and others like them) will build the core of your brand. All of your future branding decisions should expand on these ideas. Your company name, company logo, and website design should all grow from the concepts you laid out here. So, take the time to think really think about your brand from the start. Consulting is a fast-growing industry. But, it's the consulting practices with authentic brands that will survive and thrive. And if you already started your consulting business but struggling to grow it, maybe it's time to consider a rebrand. It's possible that your existing branding is holding you back more than you think. Before you decide that you should delay building a strong brand identity because you might not have a vast budget, rethink that plan. You don't have to spend thousands of dollars on building a strong brand identity. Here are a few pricing guides that can help you identify the sweet spot for pricing:

- How much should a logo design cost?
- How much does a business card cost?
- How much should brochure design cost?
- How much does website design cost?

The above guides cover free, cheap, affordable, and expensive options. You'll find a price point that will fit your budget, regardless of the size of your budget.

STEP 9

Fill In the business blanks

Once you define your brand, you can begin to think about the vitally important details of actually starting and running a consulting business. Between choosing a business structure, pricing, licensing and permits, and business plans...

There's a lot to think about.

We already covered the requirement that you have to choose the legal business structure for your new consulting business. The business structure you choose isn't a no-brainer. It will impact you and your business in the years to come.An experienced business attorney can help.

After you determine your business's legal structure, you'll need to file the necessary paperwork. The U.S. Small Business Administration tells us that some form of license or permit is necessary for virtually every business type. Their website has all of the info you need to find out what sort of license or permit you'll need to start a business in your state. Remember that most states require you to register your business if the trade name under which you operate your business differs from the legal business name.

Plan for all of the necessary legal and logistical business considerations, and you'll create a strong foundation for your consulting business's successful future.

STEP 10

Crunch the numbers

When starting any new business, it's essential to understand the numbers. But not all numbers are equally important to all businesses.

For a consulting business, you'll want to track your sales and profits, but there's so much more to think about before you can get there. You've got to start at the beginning with your start-up costs.

These costs may include:

- your brand design (logo, business cards, and website)
- any license or permit fees
- deposits and rent for a physical work location (if you plan to lease your own office space)
- basic infrastructural costs like phone and internet service, scheduling and invoicing software, etc...
- marketing and advertising costs

Once you know how much it will cost to get started, compare it with your actual funds. Then plan how you'll make up any difference. Running intelligent calculations to determine how much it will cost to run your business will allow you to plan and think about pricing.

Setting Your Fees

To create an innovative and effective fee structure, you have to start by knowing how much it costs you to run your business your operating costs. While there may always be unexpected expenses, your rent, phone bill, internet fees, invoicing software subscription or membership fees, annual taxes, supply costs, and employee salaries (if any) should all be taken into account.

But, your operating costs are only a starting point. It's essential to bake some profit into your fees as well. Otherwise, it will be challenging to sustain your business over time. You may dream of owning your brick-and-mortar consulting agency or maybe you fantasize about working from a home office or even traveling while you consult with clients around the world. Either way, for a consulting business to scale and grow, you must charge rates that support the style of business you choose to run.

There are several different strategies you can employ to achieve this goal. Andrea Coutu of Consulting Journal will walk you through your options.

Once you've done the math, it's time to start considering the less-tangible aspects of pricing competitor pricing and perceived value.

The Competition and Perceived Value

Your potential clients are most likely doing research – and they're considering your competitors, too. Consciously or not, they gather data about what they think services like yours should cost and what they're willing to pay.That means you need to be aware of what your competitors are charging, too. You might feel that your services are worth more or that you want to charge new clients less than your competitors. And that's okay. But, if you're entirely unaware of what your competitors charge, you may miss the mark completely either costing you profit if you charge too little or sales if you charge too much.

Perceived value is the amount that a customer thinks a service (or product) is worth. And, your competitor's prices are a part of that perception. But, not the whole picture. Your time has value, and you need to make a living wage. But your clients and potential clients won't care about that. They will care about the tangible results that your services deliver for their business. The more they stand to gain, the higher the perceived value.

Your branding can influence how your consulting services are perceived, as well.

A classy logo and high-end brand positioning will lead to a higher perceived value than discount brand positioning. Clients, especially new clients, may be willing to pay more if they trust your consulting brand more. So, remember to consider your brand and your competitor's pricing when creating your pricing strategy.

Ultimately, consultants charge for their services in one of three ways:

Hourly rate

An hourly rate is a flat rate, paid for each hour you work. It's based on your expertise, and clients pay only for the time (total number of hours) you spend working for them. You must track your hours using this approach, and clients will likely have questions if the work you do takes much longer than you estimated.

Project rate

A project rate offers clients an all-inclusive price based on the scope of work on a project-by-project basis. You take the risk that the work will take longer than anticipated. Project rates can work well if it takes you less time to complete the project but can create friction with changes to work scope and adjust the project rate to reflect scope changes.

Retainer

A retainer is a fixed sum of money a client will pay you per month, week, or day. This type of rate is ideal when you're providing an ongoing service to a client that can't be precisely defined by time or varies from week to week or month to month but usually within a reasonable range.

Build an online presence

Your website is one of your consulting brand's most important ambassadors.As previously explained :

Today, it's impossible to reach most customers without a website. This is especially true for new small businesses and startups trying to compete in an increasingly noisy world. but it's also true for even established companies. Don't believe me? A recent study shows that 97% of consumers research their purchases online before they buy something. Your website is a crucial component of your marketing and branding strategy.

So, put this vital business tool to work for your consulting business.Start by ensuring that your website design truly embodies your consulting brand. Visitors should understand who you are and what your brand is about as soon as they arrive. Your website's visual design and marketing copy should project your brand's voice and identity. Here are some suggestions:

- Use your brand's colors.
- Prominently feature your company logo.
- Write marketing copy with your target audience in mind.
- And showcase your personal consulting style.

Besides serving as a brand ambassador, your business website is also an excellent venue for showing off your consulting success stories to a broad audience. Consider sharing testimonials and case studies from past satisfied clients. You may even want to incorporate an online store into your website to sell your books or proprietary consulting tools Finally, a strong website design will lend credibility and legitimacy to your business. And don't worry that you have a brand new site and consulting practice. You can overcome that obstacle too. Mandi Ellefson, CEO of The Hands-Off CEO, told us that:

I could take a brand-new company and spin up a website and a logo and make it look like they've been around for 10 years. I remember doing this for a consultant and because I helped him create this brand image for him, he was able to book himself a solid list of clients in a matter of a few months.

STEP 12

Create a sales plan

There's more to a consulting business than getting a logo and creating a website. Your new business is sadly not like the field of dreams. You will need a sales strategy to bring in and close clients.

And, since a consultant is often the only member of their team, you'll need to get comfortable with selling well, yourself.If you're a sales consultant, you should already be an expert at selling.

But if your consulting business is focused on another area, you'll want to think about your sales plan and build a game plan for selling yourself and your services. Your sales plan will be the difference between success and failure.

And, this is where some practice will help you.

Take time to develop and rehearse your "elevator pitch" until you can deliver it comfortably and confidently. This 20-30 second explanation of what you do should be intriguing and dynamic.

And it should help people tell others about your consulting business. After all, the best sales channel for most consulting businesses is word of mouth referrals.

You'll also want to practice overcoming objections. No matter how excellent your services are, clients and potential clients will always have reservations – after all, their money is on the line. For example, how do you answer questions about your track record as a consultant?

So, brainstorm as many possible objections as you can think of. Then practice putting those concerns to rest.

You'll want to develop both an overall sales strategy and a list of day-to-day tactics that will keep your sales efforts moving forward. You may even want to bring in an employee or a contractor to round out your sales team.

When you're a one-or-two-man show, it's easy to let active selling fall to the wayside. But, the reality is that you don't have that luxury. Successful consulting practices build a sales pipeline, including an outside sales team that you hire on a retainer basis or commission.

If you're not selling your services, there's a good chance that no one is. So, you'll complete your current contracts to find an empty calendar and no income looming ahead of you.

Make sure to make sales a part of your day every day.

Build a mailing list and stay in touch with your clients and prospective clients.

Ultimately, you'll be writing many client proposals, so get used to doing so early in your consulting practice. Client proposals are your chance to show how you can help your client solve their problems. You'll need to be clear about the project's scope, the services you provide, what you'll charge for the services (your hourly rate and/or whether you'll work on a retainer basis), the deliverables, and the time frame. And be sure you show how you and the client will be able to measure the results.

Selling Online

You may be wondering why on earth you'd need an eCommerce store. And, maybe you don't. But if you've written a book in your field of expertise or you have your proprietary consulting materials, you may want to consider making those resources available for purchase online. Passive income can be handy for bolstering your bottom line and an important safety net for lean seasons. So here are a few things to consider if you decide to supplement your consulting income by selling online.

Most template-based web design services offer some form of e-commerce functionality. And some, like Shopify, are built specifically for e-commerce. But, think carefully before you decide to use a template-based service like Shopify.

Remember how important your unique branding is? The templates on those e-commerce sites are available for every other new consulting brand to use, as well. As we mentioned previously,

It's not enough to have a website... You also want to be sure that your site's design is unique and that it showcases your products and you.

Just like your logo, your web design should start with your personal brand. A well-designed website will expand upon and support the values and personality traits that you've identified as being core to your business. If web design is not among your many DIY skills, know that there's help available.

Self-hosted open-source e-commerce services allow you to use your own uniquely branded website with its e-commerce functionality.

Check out services like WooCommerce, Magento, and Open Cart. Not only can you use your original web design, but they also scale quickly alongside your business as it grows. And those sites also help with search engine optimization, especially if you're using a custom domain.

STEP 13

Spread the word

You may be an awesome consultant. But, if you're not marketing yourself, no one will know it. Marketing your business is the only way to ensure that you have a steady flow of clients and potential clients. It's time to focus on getting the word out about your fantastic new consulting services to your target market. One of the most effective ways to build a reputation in the consulting field and gain clients is to share your expertise with as many people as possible. John Jantsch (marketing consultant, small business marketing speaker, and bestselling author) suggests:

A central part of your prospecting should be aimed at getting in front of groups with your message get to just about any podium you can in the beginning. You'll find that speaking leads to more speaking and more speaking leads to better speaking and better speaking leads to clients.

Networking at industry events attended by your clients may also serve you well. You'll learn about industry trends and also have an opportunity to network with clients and prospective clients. Those potential word-of-mouth referrals will help drive new consulting leads.

And, also look for opportunities to attend events focused on the consulting industry. You may find that networking with others in the consulting field helps you build connections to new business sources and new clients. And you'll learn from other consultants how to develop a compelling value proposition when selling your consulting services to clients. Whenever you make personal appearances be sure to carry business cards and brochures if attendees want to learn more about your services and include a phone number and other important contact information on your business card. While many people prefer email, it isn't easy to create trust with prospective clients using email only.

The experts at Entrepreneur recommend that consultants include the following information in any marketing brochure.

A clear overview of your services

An explanation of why you are the best

A few reasons why you should be hired

A brief biography with relevant info

Some indication of who your other clients are

Content marketing is also an excellent fit for consultants.

You may consider writing an ebook about your particular field of expertise. And, blogging is another effective content marketing strategy.

Don't give away all of your secrets, of course. But, do be sure to offer valuable information from your unique perspective. Blogging and ebooks are great ways to establish authority (especially in. a niche market), build your organic search ranking through strong SEO practices, and collect email address leads.

Social Media

As a new, up-and-coming business owner, you'll also want to take full advantage of the inexpensive and easy exposure that social media marketing offers you. As we previously explained,

Social media enables you to build a social rapport with current customers, while building low-pressure relationships with future buyers.

Maintaining (at a minimum) a Twitter, Facebook, and LinkedIn presence will help you build an audience of devotees. Make it easy for visitors to see what your consulting services are all about by posting tips and observations and sharing any articles that you may have written. Establish yourself as a subject matter expert and build relationships with current and future clients by maintaining an interactive presence. This will reassure your audience that you're accessible, knowledgeable, and reliable. You can even participate in conversations on how to start a consulting business since you're becoming an expert on that topic as you run your own consulting business. Consider using a social media management tool (like Buffer) to schedule all of your social media posts ahead of time. This will allow you to build your day around your clients instead of your social media posting schedule. It's still important to check in regularly so that you can respond to any client inquiries. And consider micro-influencers who can help you in the early days. Aligning your brand with others who target your audience can help build credibility and growth. The good news is that once you've acquired your first few clients, marketing can get easier. A recent marketing strategy study for consultants revealed that "43.7% of consultants said that referrals were their highest-earning money-making marketing tactic" in 2018.

Don't be afraid to request referrals from your happy clients. They can be your most valuable marketing resource.When you're first starting, it's wise to cover as many marketing touchpoints as possible. Over time you'll learn what works best for you.

STEP 14

How to find partners or investors

One of the biggest challenges for every new business is saving enough capital to sustain and grow the business. In a perfect world, we could all fund our business ventures without any outside help. But, the truth is that most people can't do it alone. This is where business partners or outside investors can make a real difference. As with any aspect of your business, start by giving the matter some serious thought. Here are a few questions to get you started:

- What do I want to gain from this partnership or investor?
- How involved do I want them to be in the decision-making processes?

- Am I looking for a long-term or a short-term relationship?
- In any relationship, it's essential to know what you're hoping to gain.

Partner and investor relationships can come in a multitude of forms. Are you simply looking for someone to invest capital? Or are you looking for leads, someone to split costs with, or exposure and success-by-association with an established brand? Only you know what is most useful for your business. Pick the business partner you think makes the most sense. But, you should know what your goals are before meeting with any potential partner or investor. Once you've determined your relationship goals, it's time to start thinking about the type of relationship that will best meet those goals.

Here are some options for you to consider...

Crowdfunding

Crowdfunding sites like Kickstarter and Indigogo offer the opportunity to raise money from a crowd of strangers. These fundraising projects are easy to set up and allow you to raise cash without granting any investor or partner any influence over your consulting business. You will, however, need to follow through on any promises made to your backers. Reports have shown a consistent increase in crowdfunded investments since the great recession in 2008. In a recent study on the Crowdfunding Industry, World Bank predicted that the crowdfunding market could increase to between $90 and $96 billion, which is approximately 1.8 times the size of the global venture capital industry today. If you want a true business partnership, crowdfunding may not be the choice for you. And it's often not a good fit for consulting businesses. But each business, including consulting business, is unique. If you decide to give crowdfunding a try,

Angel Investors and Venture Capitalists

Angel investors and venture capitalists provide a more traditional route to raise funds for your new consulting business. If you're aiming to create a consulting agency instead of going it alone, they may be an option worth considering. But, you'll need to work hard to sell business investors on your business's financial viability.This is especially true at the beginning. Few investors are willing to invest early in a consulting business.

On the other hand, if you have a successful consulting business that you're looking to scale, it will be easier to find interested investors, especially if you're consulting in the technology space. But be prepared for investors to expect to play a significant role in your business. After all, these investors are investing their money in your consulting business in the hopes that they will make a return on that investment. So, they'll want to be sure that you're running your business in a way that is likely to ensure that return.

Partnership

Business partners can come in many forms. A true business partnership occurs when both partners invest equally in the success of the business. Both partners devote equal finances, resources, and labor to making the business work. But, if you don't already have a deeply committed partner by your side, you can also establish more casual or temporary partnerships with existing brands or other consultants. Look for brands or consultants that are complementary to your services rather than competing for your business. And make sure that you share the same goals for your partnership.

Here are two examples...

Example #1

Who: Partner with a consultant in a related field.

What: To offer your complementary services as a team.

Why: To offer more value to clients and reach a broader client base.

Example #2

Who: Partner with a software business in your field.

What: To generate a lead exchange program.

Why: To drive well-qualified leads to each other.

There are many other creative ways to partner with an existing business or another consultant. And, as long as you and your partner have the same goals, you'll be motivated to work together to achieve them.

STEP 15

Find the right help

At times, every entrepreneur has felt like they're in it alone. And when you first start your consulting business, there's a good chance that you will be.

But, for your business to scale and grow, you're going to need help. After all, there are only 24 hours in a day, and you can't work all of them. Eventually, if all goes well, you'll hire employees to take tasks off of your plate so that you can focus on serving your clients. But employees must be paid. So, at first, you should only hire for positions that will provide the most immediate benefit to your business. There's no one right answer for what those positions might be every consulting business is different. But when thinking about what positions to hire for, consider what aspects of the business are posing the most significant challenges.

And consider your limitations.

If you're a newbie to marketing, consider hiring a marketing manager to help you strategize your business.

If you're not confident about invoicing and numbers, hire a billing specialist to manage accounts and ensure payments are collected.

Hire an employee who is an expert in those areas in which your business is currently lacking. Building a robust and well-rounded team will create a stable foundation for your business.

So, what does your business need?

You may want your very first hire to be a part-time assistant. Look for someone who is a jack-of-all-trades, eager to learn new skills, and with a strong work ethic. You'll sleep better knowing you've got someone in the trenches with you that you can rely on.

The Legal Stuff

Of course, hiring staff for your consulting business means that you'll have to deal with all sorts of legalities and paperwork. This isn't an area where you should really "wing it." So, we went straight to the source. The hiring experts at Indeed recommend that you:

- Get an Employer Identification Number (EIN) by applying on the IRS website (you'll get your number immediately after applying!).
- Register with your state's labor department.
- Fill out paperwork to withhold federal taxes from your employee's wages.
- Set up workers' compensation insurance if it is required in your state.
- You'll also need to decide whether you're hiring full or part-time employees.
- Part-time employees cost less. So you may want to start with part-timers. As the business grows and you can afford it, you can expand their hours.

www.ingramcontent.com/pod-product-compliance
Lightning Source LLC
Chambersburg PA
CBHW072331290526
45794CB00002B/829